Poptails

Poptails

OVER 40 **ALCOHOL-INFUSED**
POPSICLES, ICES, AND SLUSHES

LAURA FYFE

An Hachette UK Company
www.hachette.co.uk

First published in Great Britain in 2013 by Spruce
a division of Octopus Publishing Group Ltd
Endeavour House, 189 Shaftesbury Avenue, London,
WC2H 8JY
www.octopusbooks.co.uk
www.octopusbooksusa.com

Distributed in the USA by Hachette Book Group USA
237 Park Avenue, New York, NY 10017, USA

Distributed in Canada by Canadian Manda Group
165 Dufferin Street, Toronto, Ontario, Canada,
M6K 3H6

ISBN 978-1-84601-438-3

Printed and bound in China

10 9 8 7 6 5 4 3 2 1

Consultant Publisher Sarah Ford
Copy Editor Nicole Foster
Design Eoghan O'Brien and Clare Barber
Photographer Lis Parsons
Food Styling Laura Fyfe
Production Controller Sarah Kramer

Contents

Introduction 6

Fruity 10

Shaken and Stirred 34

Ice Cream and Yogurt 48

Index 64

Introduction

Welcome to the slightly tipsy world of poptails.
Whether you're new to the notion of spiking your
pops or are a seasoned frozen cocktail pro, this book
is bound to be a source of inspiration to lead you on
to hours of poptail fun. These little frozen delights
are the perfect dessert if you've been grilling out on
a beautiful sunny evening, helping you cool down and
unwind. They are versatile too and can be transformed
into a more elegant granita or even a drinkable slush if you
desire. They offer all the refreshment of an ice cream but in
a slightly more grownup way—just be sure the kids don't get
their little mitts on them!

Molds and Variations

The recipes are all based on popsicle molds of about ½ cup
(100 ml). If you can't find any exactly this size, don't fret as you
can use larger molds and simply not fill them completely or use
smaller molds and make more. Always remember though that on
filling the molds you want to leave a little space to allow for the
poptails to expand a bit during freezing. To remove the poptails,
simply run a little hot water on the outside of the containers and
pull out with the sticks. Get creative! Nothing is set in stone—you can
use virtually any freezable hygienic container you can get your hands
on. Why not try plastic cups? Or make the Pomegranate, Vanilla, and Vodka
(see pages 28–9) in an ice cube tray and drop a few cubes into a glass of
sparkling water to make a small aperitif. For a granita, follow the recipe
instructions, but rather than filling popsicle molds, pour into a suitable-
sized freezer-safe container and cover. Every couple of hours while freezing
use a fork to break it up a bit—see the Mulled Wine Granita on page 40 to
get an idea of the texture you're after. Another option is to make slushes, sort
of like a frozen margarita. Freeze these in a container for about 4 hours, stirring
every hour to help freeze evenly. Then pour into ice-cold glasses and serve.

Ingredients

It goes without saying that the quality of your ingredients is paramount to the deliciousness of your poptail. For those that are fruit based, use the freshest fruit you can find and squeeze the juice straight from the lemon; no cheating with bottled lemon juice, please. Using traditionally crafted liquor is preferable to own brands, and when it comes to the ice creams, use free range eggs and organic milk and cream whenever possible.

Sugar Syrups

Superfine sugar is the one to use in all the recipes. Timings for making the syrup are indicated throughout, but you can't take this as gospel, as there are so many variables—mainly size of pan and how hot the burner is. You are aiming to get the syrup to a "short thread" stage, which basically means that if you place a little syrup in between your thumb and index finger (being careful not to burn yourself, as the syrup will be hot) and lift your index finger away, you should see a little short thread of syrup being pulled up. Alternatively, on a candy thermometer the temperature should read 230°F (110°C).

Other things to look out for when making a sugar syrup are not to let any sugar stick to the side of the pan and not to bring it to a boil before all the sugar has dissolved. Doing either of these things will cause the sugar to crystallize. If any sugar does stick to the side of the saucepan, use a wet pastry brush to remove it. As for dissolving the sugar, just heat it over a very low temperature—it will do no harm to give it a little gentle stir. Once it has dissolved you can bring it to a boil as quickly as you desire, but in these recipes the simmering times are based on the syrup being kept over a very low temperature with bubbles gently breaking the surface, otherwise there's a risk of ending up with a gloopy syrup that won't mix so well with the rest of the ingredients.

Makes about 3 cups (750 ml)
Preparation time: 15 minutes
+ 30 minutes infusing
+ 1 hour cooling
+ about 20 minutes churning
Freezing time: 3–5 hours

....

Ingredients

1 cup (250 ml) milk
1 cup (250 ml) heavy cream
1 vanilla bean, split
5 egg yolks
¼ cup (50 g) superfine sugar

Vanilla Ice Cream Base

Place the milk, heavy cream, and vanilla bean in a small saucepan and gently bring to a boil. Remove from the heat and let infuse for 30 minutes.

Remove the vanilla bean, scrape out the seeds, and add them back into the milk and cream mixture, discarding the pod.

Whisk together the egg yolks and sugar in a large bowl and gradually pour in the milk mixture, whisking as you pour.

Return the mixture to a clean saucepan and heat gently, stirring all the time, until it thickens enough to coat the back of a wooden spoon.

Pour into a clean bowl and cover the surface with plastic wrap (so a skin doesn't form). Let cool completely.

Pour into an ice cream machine and churn according to the manufacturer's directions. Alternatively, if you don't have a machine, place in a covered container in the freezer and beat the mixture every 30 minutes to get rid of any graininess which would otherwise spoil the finished texture. Keep freezing and beating until it becomes a smooth ice cream consistency. Then store in the freezer and use as described in the recipes.

Fruity

Makes 6
Preparation time: 10 minutes
Freezing time: 6 hours

Ingredients

2½ cups (375 g) chopped cucumber
1 cup (250 ml) elderflower cordial
½ cup (120 ml) gin

Gin Zing

An all-time favorite combination for a summer cocktail has to be gin and elderflower. Add cucumber to the mix and it zings with freshness.

Place the cucumber and elderflower cordial in a food processor or blender and blitz until smooth.

Pass the mixture through a fine strainer into a bowl and stir half of the pulp in the sieve back into the cucumber and elderflower juice. Mix in the gin until well combined, then pour into six popsicle molds.

Place the molds in the freezer. Let set for 3 hours, give it a good stir, insert the popsicle sticks, and allow to freeze until solid (about 4 more hours) or leave overnight.

Makes 6
Preparation time: 15 minutes
+ 30 minutes cooling
Freezing time: 6 hours

Ingredients

¼ cup (50 g) superfine sugar
grated zest of 1 lime
⅓ cup (75 ml) lime juice
(from 3–4 limes)
1½ cups (350 ml) apple juice
6 tablespoons vodka

Raging Bull

Use whichever is your favorite vodka for this poptail.

Put the sugar and lime zest in a saucepan with ½ cup (120 ml) water. Place over low heat and slowly let the sugar dissolve. Once it has dissolved, bring to a boil and let simmer for 5 minutes. Remove from the heat and let cool for 30 minutes.

Combine the cooled lime syrup with the lime juice, apple juice, and vodka Pour into six popsicle molds.

Place the molds in the freezer. Let set for 2 hours, insert the popsicle sticks, and allow to freeze until solid (about 4 more hours) or leave overnight.

Serves 6 as a slush
Preparation time: 10 minutes
Freezing time: 6 hours

....

Ingredients

½ cup (125 g) superfine sugar
grated zest of 1 lime
1/3 cup (75 ml) lime juice
(from 3–4 limes)
2 cups (300 g) chopped watermelon
6 tablespoons tequila
2 tablespoons Grand Marnier
2 tablespoons agave nectar

The Jaliscito

Fresh, tropical, and full of Mexican color.
This poptail is really delicious served as a slush.

Put the sugar and lime zest in a saucepan with 1 cup (250 ml) water. Place over low heat. Gently bring to a simmer, allowing the sugar to dissolve. Let bubble gently for 5 minutes, remove from the heat, and pour in the lime juice.

Place the chopped watermelon in a food processor or blender, add the lime syrup, tequila, Grand Marnier, and agave nectar and blitz until well combined.

Pour into a freezer-safe container, cover, and place in the freezer for up to 6 hours, giving it a good stir every 2 hours. Remove from the freezer, blitz in a food processor or blender, and pour into glasses. Allow to thaw a little (approxmately 10 minutes), then serve.

Makes 8
Preparation time: 1 hour
(including cooling)
Freezing time: 6 hours

Ingredients

¼ cup (50 g) superfine sugar
2 plums, quartered and
pits removed
2 tablespoons gin
2 tablespoons Grand Marnier
1 cup (250 ml) ginger ale

Red Velvet

If you can't find any fresh plums, this would work nicely
with peaches or nectarines too.

Place the sugar, plums, and ½ cup (120 ml) water in a saucepan. Bring
slowly to a boil and allow to bubble for 5–10 minutes until the plums
are completely soft. Let cool completely.

Place the cooled plums and syrup in a blender or food processor and blitz
until smooth. Pass through a fine sieve and stir in the rest of the ingredients.
Pour into eight popsicle molds.

Place the molds in the freezer. Let set for 2 hours, insert the popsicle sticks,
and allow to freeze until solid (about 4 more hours).

Makes 4
Preparation time: 10 minutes
Freezing time: 6 hours

Ingredients

¼ cup (50 g) superfine sugar
2 cups (400 g) chopped pineapple
4 tablespoons lime juice
4 tablespoons rum
¼ cup (20 g) mint leaves

Pineapple Mojito

To peel the pineapple, cut off the base and stand the
pineapple upright on a board, then use your knife
to cut away the skin downwards.

Place the sugar and ½ cup (120 ml) water in a saucepan and slowly bring
up to a boil, allowing the sugar to dissolve. Let simmer for 5 minutes,
then remove from the heat.

Place the chopped pineapple in a food processor or blender and blitz until
completely smooth. Add the sugar syrup, lime juice, and rum and blitz until
well combined. Coarsely chop any larger mint leaves, but leave the smaller
ones intact. Stir the mint through the pineapple mix and pour into four
popsicle molds.

Place the molds in the freezer. Let set for 2 hours, insert the popsicle sticks,
and allow to freeze until completely solid (about 4 more hours).

Makes 6
Preparation time: 10 minutes
Freezing time: 6 hours

Ingredients

½ cup (125 g) superfine sugar
½ cup (75 g) pomegranate seeds
(from 1 pomegranate)
1 cup (250 ml) prosecco
1 tablespoon rose water

Flamingo-go

To remove the seeds from the pomegranate, bash it with a wooden spoon while it's still whole. This will loosen them from the shell and make them easier to pick off.

Place the sugar and 1 cup (250 ml) water in a saucepan and slowly bring to a boil, allowing the sugar to dissolve. Let simmer for 5 minutes, then remove from the heat.

Stir in the pomegranate seeds, prosecco, and rose water. Pour into six popsicle molds.

Place the molds in the freezer. After 3 hours give each one a gentle stir to distribute the pomegranate seeds and insert the popsicle sticks. Return to the freezer for an additional 3 hours, until frozen solid.

Makes 2
Preparation time: 20 minutes
Freezing time: 6 hours

Ingredients

2 apples, peeled, cored and
cut into cubes
¼ cup (50 g) superfine sugar
2 tablespoons vermouth
3 tablespoons gin

Appletini Mojito

When cutting up the apples, squeeze over a little lemon juice to prevent them from going brown.

Put the apple cubes and sugar in a small saucepan with 1 cup (250 ml) water. Slowly bring to a boil, allowing the sugar to dissolve. Let bubble gently for 15 minutes, until the apples are completely soft, then remove from the heat.

Pour the apple mixture into a food processor or blender and blitz until very smooth. Pass through a fine strainer, then stir in the vermouth and gin. Pour into two popsicle molds.

Place the molds in the freezer. Let set for 2 hours, insert the popsicle sticks, and allow to freeze until completely solid (about 4 more hours).

Makes 4
Preparation time: 15 minutes
Freezing time: 6 hours

....

Ingredients

½ cup (125 g) superfine sugar
grated zest of 1 lime
½ cup (125 ml) passion fruit pulp
(about 6 passion fruit)
⅓ cup (75 ml) lime juice
2 tablespoons tequila
1 tablespoon Cointreau

Passion Fruit Margarita

When removing the seeds from the passion fruit, be sure not to lose any of the delicious juice.

Place the sugar and lime zest in a small saucepan with 1 cup (250 ml) water. Slowly bring to a boil, allowing the sugar to dissolve. Let bubble for 5 minutes, then remove from the heat.

Stir in the remaining ingredients and pour into four popsicle molds.

Place the molds in the freezer. After 3 hours give each one a gentle stir to distribute the passion fruit seeds and insert the popsicle sticks. Return to the freezer for an additional 3 hours, until frozen solid.

Makes 6
Preparation time: 15 minutes
Freezing time: 4 hours

···

Ingredients

¼ cup (50 g) superfine sugar
1 cup (250 ml) prosecco
2 cups (250 g) frozen raspberries

Raspberry Bellini

This is a twist on the classic peach bellini. Using frozen raspberries will help the drink freeze faster. Freeze for 2 hours, then eat with a teaspoon.

Place the sugar and ½ cup (125 ml) water in a small saucepan and slowly bring to a boil, allowing the sugar to dissolve. Let simmer for 5 minutes, then remove from the heat. Stir the syrup into the prosecco and allow to cool.

Place the frozen raspberries in a food processor and add the prosecco mixture. Blitz until smooth and then pour into six popsicle molds.

Place the molds in the freezer. Let set for 2 hours, insert the popsicle sticks, and allow to freeze until completely solid (about 2 more hours).

Makes 4
Preparation time: 30 minutes
(including cooling)
Freezing time: 6 hours

···

Ingredients

¼ cup (50 g) superfine sugar
2 star anise
1 cup (250 ml) freshly squeezed orange juice (about 3 oranges)
4 tablespoons Cointreau

Cointreau, Orange juice, and Star Anise

The longer you leave the star anise in the syrup the stronger it will be, so for an extra aniseed kick, make the syrup a few hours before you need it.

Place the sugar and star anise in a small saucepan with ½ cup (125 ml) water. Slowly bring to a boil, allowing the sugar to dissolve. Let simmer gently for 5 minutes, then remove from the heat and add the rest of the ingredients. Allow to cool completely.

Once cool, remove the star anise and pour into popsicle molds.

Place the molds in the freezer. Let set for 2 hours, insert the popsicle sticks, and allow to freeze until completely solid (about 4 more hours).

Makes 6
Preparation time: 10 minutes
Freezing time: 8 hours

Ingredients

½ cup (125 g) superfine sugar
3 tablespoons pomegranate juice
2 cups (500 ml) orange juice
6 tablespoons rum

Caribbean Sunrise

A twist on the Tequila Sunrise, using rum to add that Caribbean flavor.

Place the sugar and 1 cup (250 ml) water in a saucepan and slowly bring to a boil, allowing the sugar to dissolve. Let simmer gently for 5 minutes then remove from the heat.

Combine 2 tablespoons of the sugar syrup with the pomegranate juice and divide the mixture among six popsicle molds. Place in the freezer for 2 hours. Combine the remaining sugar syrup with the orange juice and rum and let cool completely.

After 2 hours remove the molds from the freezer and pour the orange juice mixture over the pomegranate base.

Return the molds to the freezer. After 2 hours insert the popsicle sticks and allow to freeze until completely solid (about 4 more hours).

Makes 6
Preparation time: 10 minutes
Freezing time: 6 hours

Ingredients

½ cup (125 g) superfine sugar
½ teaspoon vanilla extract
6 tablespoons dark rum
2 cups (300 g) chopped
cantaloupe melon

Melon Daiquiri

This one is also delicious as a slush or a granita. If you can't find a cantaloupe melon, honeydew would make a nice substitute.

Place the sugar and 1 cup (250 ml) water in a saucepan and slowly bring to a boil, allowing the sugar to dissolve. Let simmer gently for 5 minutes, then remove from the heat and stir in the vanilla extract and rum.

Place the melon cubes in a food processor or blender, and pour the syrup over. Blitz, until completely smooth, then pour into six popsicle molds.

Place the molds in the freezer. Let set for 2 hours, insert the popsicle sticks, and allow to freeze until completely solid (about 4 more hours).

Makes 4
Preparation time: 20 minutes
Freezing time: 4½ hours

....

Ingredients

½ cup (125 g) superfine sugar
½ cup (60 g) blueberries
2 tablespoons blue curaçao
½ cup (250 g) chopped mango
2 tablespoons tequila
½ cup (100 g) chopped strawberries
2 tablespoons dark rum

Tropical Rainbow

This is an impressive three-layered popsicle. Make sure each layer is completely frozen before adding the next, as it looks great when the layers are really well defined.

Place the sugar and 1 cup (250 ml) water in a saucepan and slowly bring to a boil, allowing the sugar to dissolve. Let simmer gently for 5 minutes, then remove from the heat.

Place the blueberries in a food processor and add the blue curaçao and one-third of the sugar syrup (about 5 tablespoons). Blitz until completely smooth, then pour into the bottom of four popsicle molds and place in the freezer for 1½ hours.

Meanwhile, clean the food processor bowl and add the mango with the tequila and another one-third of the syrup. Blitz until completely smooth.

When the blueberry base is frozen solid, remove the molds from the freezer and pour over the mango mixture. Return the molds to the freezer and freeze for another 1½ hours.

Finally, blitz together the strawberries, rum, and remaining syrup. Pour the strawberry mixture over the mango layer once it has frozen solid.

Freeze for another 1½ hours, or until completely solid.

Makes 4
Preparation time: 15 minutes
+ 30 minutes infusing
Freezing time: 6 hours

....

Ingredients

½ vanilla bean
¼ cup (50 g) superfine sugar
1½ cups (350 ml) pomegranate juice
4 tablespoons vodka

Pomegranate, Vanilla, and Vodka

This is best made with a vanilla bean, as you get flecks of seeds through the popsicle, but if you can't get your hands on any, replace with 1 teaspoon vanilla extract (no need to allow it to infuse).

Scrape the seeds from the vanilla bean and place both pod and seeds in a saucepan with the sugar and ½ cup (125 ml) water. Slowly bring to a boil, allowing the sugar to dissolve. Let simmer gently for 5 minutes, then remove from the heat. Allow to infuse for 30 minutes.

Remove the vanilla pod from the syrup and mix in the pomegranate juice and vodka. Pour into four popsicle molds.

Place the molds in the freezer. Let set for 2 hours, insert the popsicle sticks, and allow to freeze until completely solid (about 4 more hours).

Makes 4
Preparation time: 10 minutes
Freezing time: 6 hours

....

Ingredients

¼ cup (50 g) superfine sugar
1 cup (250 ml) orange juice
4 tablespoons Campari
4 tablespoons prosecco

The Milanese

If you're reluctant to open a bottle of prosecco for just 4 tablespoons, it can easily be substituted with a nice fruity white wine.

Place the sugar and ½ cup (125 ml) water in a saucepan and slowly bring to a boil, allowing the sugar to dissolve. Let simmer gently for 5 minutes, then remove from the heat.

Stir the remaining ingredients into the syrup and pour into four popsicle molds.

Place the molds in the freezer. Let set for 2 hours, insert the popsicle sticks, and allow to freeze until completely solid (about 4 more hours).

Makes 4
Preparation time: 15 minutes
Freezing time: 6 hours

....

Ingredients

¼ cup (50 g) superfine sugar
1 cup (200 g) chopped tomatoes
1 cup (150 g) chopped cucumber
4 tablespoons vodka

Gazpacho

This one is more savory, so perhaps best served before a meal as a little aperitif.

Place the sugar and ½ cup (125 ml) water in a small saucepan and slowly bring to a boil, allowing the sugar to dissolve. Let simmer gently for 5 minutes, then remove from the heat.

Place the tomatoes, cucumber, and vodka in a food processor or blender, and blitz until completely smooth. Add the sugar syrup and blitz until well combined. Pour into four popsicle molds.

Place the molds in the freezer. Let set for 2 hours, insert the popsicle sticks, and allow to freeze until completely solid (about 4 more hours).

Makes 4
Preparation time: 1 hour
(including cooling)
Freezing time: 6 hours

....

Ingredients

1½ cups (150 g) chopped apple
1 cinnamon stick
Pinch of ground cinnamon
¼ cup (50 g) superfine sugar
1 cup (250 ml) hard cider

Autumn Orchard

Be sure to blend the apples and cider into a really smooth mixture. For a more delicate texture you might want to pass the mixture through a sieve.

Place the chopped apple, cinnamon stick, and ground cinnamon in a saucepan and pour over the sugar and 1 cup (250 ml) water. Slowly bring to a boil, allowing the sugar to dissolve. Let simmer gently for 15 minutes then remove from the heat and allow to cool completely.

When it has cooled, remove the cinnamon stick and place the apple mixture in a food processor or blender with the cider. Blitz until completely smooth and pour into four popsicle molds.

Place the molds in the freezer. Let set for 2 hours, insert the popsicle sticks, and allow to freeze until completely solid (about 4 more hours).

Makes 4
Preparation time: 15 minutes
Freezing time: 6 hours

Ingredients

¼ cup (50 g) superfine sugar
1 cup (200 g) quartered strawberries
2 tablespoons vodka
2 tablespoons Cointreau
½ cup (125 ml) soda water

Strawberry Cosmopolitan

The strawberries are crushed rather than blended, which gives the popsicle a very satisfying texture—just delicious.

Place the sugar and ½ cup (125 ml) water in a small saucepan. Let the sugar dissolve over low heat, then bring it to a boil. Remove from the heat.

Add the strawberries to the pan. Squash the strawberries into the syrup using the back of a fork or a pestle, but allowing some texture to remain. Pour in the remaining ingredients and divide the mixture among four popsicle molds.

Place the molds in the freezer. Let set for 2 hours, insert the popsicle sticks, and allow to freeze until completely solid (about 4 more hours).

Makes 4
Preparation time: 1 hour
(including cooling)
Freezing time: 6 hours

Ingredients

½ cup (125 ml) limoncello
¼ cup (50 g) superfine sugar
3 sprigs basil
1½ cups (300 g) coarsely chopped tomatoes

The Italian Job

You need to make sure that the ingredients are really well combined before freezing. And give the molds a good stir or two while in the freezer, otherwise the limoncello has a tendency to rise to the surface.

Place the limoncello, sugar, and basil sprigs in a small saucepan with ½ cup (125 ml) water and slowly bring to a boil. Let simmer for 5 minutes, then remove from the heat and allow to cool completely.

Put the tomatoes in a food processor or blender and blitz until very smooth. Add the cooled syrup and blitz until really well combined. Pour into four popsicle molds.

Place the molds in the freezer for 2 hours, then remove and give the mixture a stir. Insert the popsicle sticks and freeze for an additional 4 hours until completely solid.

Shaken
and
Stirred

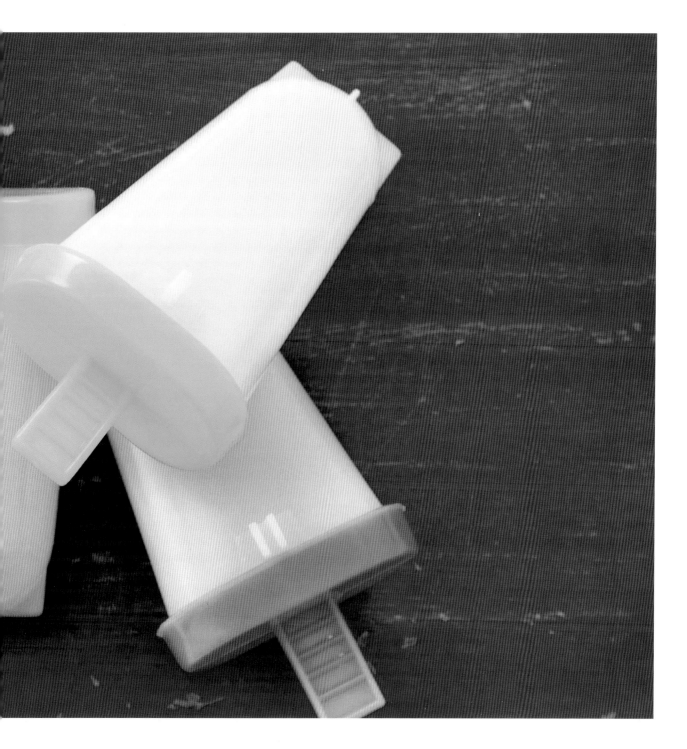

Makes 2
Preparation time: 10 minutes
Freezing time: 6 hours

Ingredients

3 tablespoons superfine sugar
½ cup (125 ml) strong
espresso, cooled
2 tablespoons gin

Espresso Martini

It's nice to serve these as a slush in espresso cups or to make smaller ones as a nice after dinner treat with coffee.

Place the sugar and 4 tablespoons water in a small saucepan. Let the sugar dissolve over low heat, then bring to a boil. Remove from the heat and pour into a cocktail shaker.

Strain the cooled espresso through a fine sieve. Add the gin and espresso to the cocktail shaker and shake well. Pour into two popsicle molds.

Place the molds in the freezer. Let set for 2 hours, insert the popsicle sticks, and allow to freeze until completely solid (about 4 more hours).

Makes 6
Preparation time: 5 minutes
Freezing time: 6 hours

Ingredients

2 tablespoons honey
4 tablespoons whiskey
2 cups (500 ml) ginger beer

Bees Knees

This is very simple to make. It's a good idea to stir it every so often during the freezing stage to help break up the ice crystals.

Put the honey and whiskey into a bowl and, using a small whisk, mix together until well combined. Gradually whisk in the ginger beer, making sure that everything is thoroughly blended.

Pour into six popsicle molds and place in the freezer. After 2 hours give each one a good stir. Freeze for another 2 hours, stir, and insert the popsicle sticks. Return to the freezer and freeze for another 2 hours, until completely solid.

Makes 4
Preparation time: 10 minutes
Freezing time: 8–10 hours

....

Ingredients

½ cup (125 ml) lemon juice
½ cup (125 g) superfine sugar
4 tablespoons tequila
½ cup (125 ml) soda water
1 tablespoon crème de cassis

Tequila Sunrise

When you pour the cassis mixture into the molds you want it to float on top and slightly blend in with the tequila base. So the tequila needs to be almost frozen, but still a little slushy.

Place the lemon juice and sugar in a saucepan with ½ cup (125 ml) water and slowly bring to a boil, allowing the sugar to dissolve. Let bubble for 5 minutes, then remove from the heat.

Pour in the tequila and soda water and mix well to combine. Measure out 6 tablespoons of the mixture and set aside. Divide the remaining mixture among four popsicle molds. Place the molds in the freezer for 4 hours.

Combine the reserved mixture with the cassis. After the 4 hours are up, remove the popsicles from the freezer and pour the cassis mixture into the molds. Insert the popsicle sticks and freeze for another 4–6 hours, until completely solid.

Serves 4
Preparation time: 20 minutes
+ 1 hour cooling
Freezing time: 6–8 hours

Ingredients

¼ cup (50 g) superfine sugar
½ cup (125 ml) water
2 cups (500 ml) red wine
1 cinnamon stick
3 cloves
3 allspice berries
1 strip of orange zest

Mulled Wine Granita

This is a wintery poptail. Give your guests a choice and serve it alongside the Eggnog popsicle on page 54.

Place all the ingredients in a saucepan and slowly bring to a boil, allowing the sugar to dissolve. Gently simmer for 15 minutes. Remove from the heat and let cool completely, approximately 1 hour.

Pour the cooled mixture into a rectangular dish, cover, and freeze for 6–8 hours, stirring it with a fork every 2 hours. Give one final stir before serving.

Makes 6
Preparation time: 10 minutes
Freezing time: 6 hours

Ingredients

¼ cup (50 g) superfine sugar
4 tablespoons lime juice
1 can (1¼ cups/330 ml) Mexican beer
½ cup (125 ml) lemonade
few drops of Tabasco (optional)

Mexican Shandy

It's fun to go the extra mile and garnish the base of the popsicles with a little salt, like margarita glasses. You can do this once they've been removed from the molds.

Place the sugar, lime juice, and 4 tablespoons water in a small saucepan and slowly bring to a boil, allowing the sugar to dissolve. Let bubble for 5 minutes, then remove from the heat.

Add the beer, lemonade, and Tabasco (if using), and stir to combine, then pour into six popsicle molds.

Place the molds in the freezer. Let set for 2 hours, insert the popsicle sticks, and allow to freeze until completely solid (about 4 more hours).

Makes 4
Preparation time: 15 minutes
+ 30 minutes cooling
Freezing time: 6 hours

Ingredients

½ cup (125 g) superfine sugar
grated zest of 1 lime
cup (75 ml) lime juice
½ cup (125 ml) ginger beer
4 tablespoons rum

Dark and Stormy

If you use a zester to pare the lime zest (rather than a grater), you will end up with nice strands of lime that soften in the syrup and taste delicious.

Place the sugar and lime zest in a saucepan with 1 cup (250 ml) water and slowly bring to a boil, allowing the sugar to dissolve. Let simmer gently for 5 minutes, then remove from the heat and add the rest of the ingredients. Let cool completely.

Pour into four popsicle molds and place in the freezer. After 2 hours, remove from the freezer and stir to distribute the lime zest. Insert the popsicle sticks. Allow to freeze until completely solid (about 4 more hours).

Makes 4
Preparation time: 15 minutes
+ 30 minutes infusing
Freezing time: 6 hours

Ingredients

¼ cup (125 g) grated
fresh gingerroot
½ cup (125 g) superfine sugar
6 tablespoons whiskey
2 tablespoons orange blossom water
1 cup (250 ml) soda water
Grated zest of ½ orange

Highland Fling

If you can't get hold of any orange blossom water, try replacing it with some orange juice.

Put the ginger and sugar in a small saucepan and cover with 1 cup (250 ml) water. Place over low heat until the sugar has dissolved. Once it has dissolved, bring to a boil and let simmer for 5 minutes. Remove from the heat and allow to infuse for 30 minutes.

Combine the ginger syrup with the whiskey, orange blossom water, soda water, and orange zest. Pour into four popsicle molds.

Place the molds in the freezer. After 3 hours remove from the freezer and stir to distribute the orange zest. Insert the popsicle sticks and freeze until solid (about 3 hours).

Makes 6
Preparation time: 30 minutes
(including cooling)
Freezing time: 6 hours

Ingredients

¼ cup (50 g) superfine sugar
4 tablespoons Pimm's
1 cup (250 ml) ginger beer
(or lemonade)
¾ cup (150 g) sliced strawberries
¼ cup (50 g) sliced apples
18 small mint leaves

English Summer Cup

There's a lot of fruit in these, which makes them perfect for a summer BBQ.

Place the sugar and ½ cup (125 ml) water in a saucepan and slowly bring to a boil, allowing the sugar to dissolve. Let simmer gently for 5 minutes, then remove from the heat.

Add the Pimm's and ginger beer or lemonade. Let cool completely.

Divide the strawberries, apple slices, and mint leaves among six popsicle molds. Pour over the Pimm's mixture and insert the popsicle sticks.

Place the molds in the freezer for 6 hours, until frozen solid.

Makes 4
Preparation time: 10 minutes
+ 30 minutes infusing
Freezing time: 6 hours

Ingredients

1 stalk lemon grass, sliced
3 sprigs mint
½ cup (125 g) superfine sugar
4 tablespoons vodka
½ cup (125 ml) lemonade
2 tablespoons shredded mint

Mint, Lemon Grass, and Vodka

After 30 minutes the syrup will have a nice subtle taste, but if you want it stronger, let the lemon grass and vodka infuse for a little longer.

Place the lemon grass, mint sprigs, and sugar in a saucepan with 1 cup (250 ml) water. Slowly bring to a boil, allowing the sugar to dissolve. Let simmer gently for 5 minutes. Remove from the heat and allow to infuse for 30 minutes.

Strain the syrup through a fine sieve into a bowl and combine with the remaining ingredients. Pour into four popsicle molds.

Place the molds in the freezer. After 2 hours, remove from the freezer and stir to distribute the mint leaves. Insert the popsicle sticks. Allow to freeze until completely solid (about 4 more hours).

Makes 6
Preparation time: 10 minutes
+ 30 minutes infusing
Freezing time: 6 hours

....

Ingredients

½ cup (125 g) superfine sugar
4 sprigs mint
2 cups (225 g) blueberries
6 tablespoons bourbon

Blueberry Julep

Use the whole mint sprigs, stalks included,
for a good minty hit.

Place the sugar and mint in a saucepan with 1 cup (250 ml) water
and slowly bring to a boil, allowing the sugar to dissolve. Let simmer
gently for 5 minutes, then remove from the heat and allow to infuse
for 30 minutes.

Place the blueberries and bourbon in a food processor or blender,
and pour over the syrup, mint sprigs included. Blitz until completely
smooth. Pour into six popsicle molds.

Place the molds in the freezer. Let set for 2 hours, insert the popsicle
sticks, and allow to freeze until completely solid (about 4 more hours).

Ice Cream and Yogurt

Makes 6
Preparation time: 25 minutes
(including softening)
Freezing time: 2 hours

Ingredients

2 cups (500 ml) coconut and lime
ice cream (see right)
¼ cup (40 g) chopped pecans
6 tablespoons rum
½ cup (40 g) shredded coconut

Coconut Crunch

This ice cream poptail combines delicious and fresh summer flavors; it reminds me of being on the beach.

For the base coconut and lime ice cream, follow the Vanilla Ice Cream Base recipe on page 8, substituting the grated zest of 2 limes for the vanilla bean, and 1 cup (250 ml) coconut milk for the heavy cream.

Remove the ice cream from the freezer and let soften for 20 minutes.

Place the ice cream in a large bowl and stir in the pecans and rum until evenly mixed. Pack into six popsicle molds, insert the sticks, and freeze until solid, about 2 hours.

Meanwhile, heat a skillet over a medium flame, and add the shredded coconut. Cook for 2–3 minutes, stirring frequently, until lightly golden.

When ready to serve, remove the popsicles from the molds and roll in the shredded coconut. Serve immediately.

Makes 6
Preparation time: 25 minutes
(including softening)
Freezing time: 2 hours

Ingredients

2 cups (500 ml) Vanilla Ice Cream
Base (see page 8)
4 tablespoons sherry

Don Pedro

You could combine the sherry with the base ice cream after the churning stage, before freezing it.

Remove the ice cream from the freezer and let soften for 20 minutes.

Place in a large bowl and swirl through the sherry. Pack into six popsicle molds, insert the sticks, and freeze until solid, about 2 hours.

Makes 6
Preparation time: 30 minutes
(including softening)
Freezing time: 2 hours

Ingredients

1 cup (125 g) blackberries
6 tablespoons amaretto
2 cups (500 ml) Vanilla Ice Cream
Base (see page 8) or store-bought
10 amaretti cookies (optional)

Muddled Blackberries, Vanilla, and Amaretto

If using homemade ice cream, the blackberries could be mixed in after the churning stage. Then you're ready to make the popsicles on the day you want to serve them.

Place the blackberries in a bowl and pour over the amaretto. Using a fork, squash the blackberries against the side of the bowl so that they are lightly crushed. Set aside for 20 minutes.

Meanwhile, remove the ice cream from the freezer so it softens a little.

After 20 minutes, combine the blackberry mixture with the ice cream and pack into six popsicle molds. Insert the popsicle sticks and freeze until solid, about 2 hours.

If using, blitz the amaretti cookies in a food processor until coarsely chopped. Remove the popsicles from the molds and roll in the amaretti crumbs. Serve immediately.

Makes 6
Preparation time: 30 minutes
(including softening)
Freezing time: 2 hours

······································

Ingredients

2 cups (500 ml) Vanilla Ice Cream
Base (see page 8)
½ cup (125 ml) coffee essence
½ cup (125 ml) whiskey

Irish Coffee

You could spoon the first layer into the molds after the ice cream has churned. To finish, combine an additional 1½ cups (350 ml) ice cream with the coffee essence and whiskey and fill the molds.

Remove the ice cream from the freezer and let soften for 10 minutes. Divide ½ cup (125 ml) among six popsicle molds, pushing it right into the tip as evenly as possible. Place the molds in the freezer while you prepare the coffee layer.

Let the remaining ice cream soften for another 10 minutes, then place in a bowl and stir in the coffee essence and whiskey.

Remove the popsicle molds from the freezer and layer the flavored ice cream on top of the frozen ice cream in the tips of the molds. Insert the popsicle sticks and freeze until solid, about 2 hours.

Makes 8
Preparation time: 15 minutes
+ 30 minutes infusing + 1 hour cooling
+ about 20 minutes churning
Freezing time: 4 hours

······································

Ingredients

1 cup (250 ml) milk
1 cup (250 ml) heavy cream
1 teaspoon grated nutmeg
5 egg yolks
¼ cup (50 g) superfine sugar
½ cup (125 ml) bourbon

Eggnog

This is a classic eggnog recipe, churned and frozen. It makes delicious, festive popsicles.

Follow the method for Vanilla Ice Cream Base on page 8, but use the grated nutmeg instead of the vanilla.

Once the ice cream has churned, stir through the bourbon, then pack into eight popsicle molds. Insert the sticks and freeze until solid, about 4 hours.

Makes 8
Preparation time: 1 hour
(including cooling)
Freezing time: 2 hours

....

Ingredients

2 cups (175 g) chopped nectarines
¼ cup (50 g) superfine sugar
8 tablespoons basil leaves
2 cups (500 ml) Vanilla Ice Cream
Base (see page 8)
½ cup (125 ml) vodka

Nectarine and Basil Ice Cream

All the vibrant flavors of midsummer combined in one hit!

Place the nectarines, sugar, and half the basil leaves in a saucepan with 2 tablespoons water. Slowly bring to a boil and cook until the nectarines are completely soft, about 15 minutes. Remove from the heat and put into a food processor. or blender Blitz until completely smooth. Allow to cool completely.

Remove the ice cream from the freezer and let soften for 20 minutes. Place in a large bowl.

Coarsely chop the remaining basil leaves. In a small bowl, combine the nectarine puree, chopped basil leaves, and vodka, then stir into the softened ice cream.

Pack into eight popsicle molds. Insert the popsicle sticks and freeze until solid, about 2 hours.

Makes 8
Preparation time: 20 minutes
+ 1 hour cooling
+ about 20 minutes churning
Freezing time: 4 hours

....

Ingredients

2 cups (500 ml) milk
1 cup (250 ml) heavy cream
1 chili pepper, chopped
1 cup (250 g) chopped chocolate
½ cup (125 ml) rum
2 egg yolks
¼ cup (50 g) superfine sugar

El Diablo

If the idea of chili in ice cream scares you, you can simply leave it out and make a chocolate rum popsicle.

Place the milk, cream, and chili in a small saucepan and bring to a boil. Remove from the heat and let sit for 5 minutes.

Place the chocolate in a heatproof bowl, pour the milk mixture over it, and stir until it has melted. Stir in the rum.

Whisk the egg yolks and sugar in a bowl and gradually pour over the chocolate mixture. Keep whisking until well combined. Cover the surface with plastic wrap and let cool completely.

Place in an ice cream machine and churn according to the manufacturer's directions.

Pack eight popsicle molds with the ice cream. Insert the sticks and freeze until solid, about 4 hours.

Makes 6
Preparation time: 5 minutes
Freezing time: 3 hours

Ingredients

4 tablespoons vodka
2 tablespoons Kahlúa
1 tablespoon honey
2½ cups (600 g) plain yogurt

White Russian

This is a very simple poptail—the quality of the ingredients is what's really going to make a difference.

Combine all the ingredients in a large bowl and use to fill six popsicle molds.

Place the molds in the freezer. Freeze for 1 hour, insert the popsicle sticks, and allow to freeze until completely solid (about 2 more hours).

Makes 4
Preparation time: 5 minutes
Freezing time: 3 hours

Ingredients

1½ cups (350 g) plain yogurt
½ cup (75 g) chopped
preserved ginger
4 tablespoons ginger syrup
4 tablespoons bourbon

Preserved Ginger

Give the yogurt a little stir after the first hour—this will help mix around the ginger and break up any ice crystals.

Combine all the ingredients in a bowl and use to fill four popsicle molds.

Place the molds in the freezer. After 1 hour, remove and give each one a gentle stir. Insert the popsicle sticks and allow to freeze until completely solid (about 2 hours).

Makes 6
Preparation time: 20 minutes
Freezing time: 3 hours

....

Ingredients

1 green tea bag
½ cup (125 ml) boiling water
4 cardamom pods
¼ cup (50 g) superfine sugar
6 tablespoons whiskey
2 cups (500 g) plain yogurt

Cardamom

For a stronger green tea flavor, let the tea bag infuse for longer.

Place the tea bag in a pitcher and pour over the water. Set aside and allow to infuse for 10 minutes. Discard the tea bag.

Lightly crush the cardamom seeds with a mortar and pestle and place in a saucepan along with the sugar. Pour over the green tea, let the sugar dissolve, then bring to a simmer and allow to bubble for 10 minutes, until you have a thick syrup.

Combine the syrup with the whiskey. Put the yogurt into a bowl, then stir through the whiskey syrup. Pour into six popsicle molds.

Place the molds in the freezer. Freeze for 1 hour, insert the popsicle sticks, and allow to freeze until completely solid (about 2 more hours).

Makes 4
Preparation time: 25 minutes
(including soaking)
Freezing time: 3 hours

....

Ingredients

¼ cup (40 g) raisins
4 tablespoons rum
2 tablespoons agave nectar
1 teaspoon ground cinnamon
1½ cups (350 g) plain yogurt

Rum and Raisin

Give the yogurt a little stir after 1 hour. This will help distribute the raisins and break up any ice crystals.

Place the raisins in a bowl and pour over the rum. Set aside and let soak for 20 minutes.

In a separate bowl, combine the agave nectar and ground cinnamon, then stir in the yogurt.

Stir the raisins and rum into the yogurt mixture and pour into four popsicle molds. Place in the freezer.

After 1 hour, remove and give each one a gentle stir. Insert the popsicle sticks and allow to freeze until completely solid (about 2 hours).

Index

Amaretto 52–3
apple
  Appletini Mojito 18
  Autumn orchard 30
  English Summer Cup 44–5
  Raging Bull 12

beer, Mexican Shandy 40
Bees Knees 36
Bellini, raspberry 22–3
blackberries 52–3
blueberries 26–7, 46–7
Blue Curaçao 26–7
bourbon 46–7, 54, 60–1

Campari, the Milanese 28
cardamom yogurt 62–3
Caribbean Sunrise 24–5
cassis, Tequila Sunrise 38–9
chili, El Diablo 58–9
chocolate, El Diablo 58–9
cider, Autumn orchard 30
coconut crunch 50–1
coffee 36–7, 54–5
Cointreau 20–1, 22–3, 32–3
cream 8, 54, 58–9
cucumber 12, 30–1

Daiquiri, melon 24
Dark and Stormy 42–3
Don Pedro 50–1

eggnog 54
eggs 8, 58–9
elderflower cordial 12
El Diablo 58–9
Espresso Martini 36–7

Flamingo-go 18–19
freezing 6

gazpacho 30–1
gin 12, 16–17, 18, 36–7
ginger
  ale, Red Velvet 16–17
  beer 36, 42–3, 44–5
  Highland Fling 42
  preserved, yogurt 60–1
Grand Marnier 14–15, 16–17
granitas 6, 24, 32–3, 40–1
green tea 62–3

Highland Fling 42
honey 36, 60–1

ice cream
  blackberry, vanilla and
    Amaretto 52–3
  coconut crunch 50–1
  Don Pedro 50–1
  eggnog 54
  El Diablo 58
  Irish coffee 54–5
  nectarine and basil
    56–7
  vanilla 8–9
ice cubes 6, 28
ingredients 7
Irish coffee 54–5
the Italian Job 32

the Jaliscito 14–15

Kahlua, White Russian 60–1

lemon, Tequila Sunrise 38–9
lemonade 40, 44–5
lemon grass 44–5
lime
  coconut crunch 50
  Dark and Stormy 42–3

the Jaliscito 14–15
Mexican Shandy 40
passion fruit Margarita 20
pineapple Mojito 16
Raging Bull 12
limoncello 32

mango, Tropical Rainbow 26–7
Margarita, passion fruit 20–1
melon Daiquiri 24
Mexican Shandy 40
the Milanese 28
milk 8, 54, 58–9
mint 16, 44, 44–5, 46–7
Mojitos 16–17, 18
molds 6

nectarine ice cream 56–7

orange 22–3, 24–5, 28
orange blossom water 42

passion fruit, Margarita 20–1
Pimms, English Summer Cup 44
pineapple, Mojito 16–17
plums, Red Velvet 16–17
pomegranate 18–19, 24–5, 28–9
prosecco 18–19, 22–3, 28

Raging Bull 12
raspberry Bellini 22–3
Red Velvet 16–17
red wine, granita 40–1
rum
  Caribbean Sunrise 24–5
  coconut crunch 50–1
  Dark and Stormy 42–3
  El Diablo 58–9
  melon Daiquiri 24
  pineapple Mojito 16

and raisin yogurt 62–3
Tropical Rainbow 26–7

sherry, Don Pedro 50–1
slush 6, 14–15, 22–3, 24
soda water 38–9, 42
star anise 22
strawberries 26–7, 32–3, 44–5
sugar syrups 7
Summer Cup, English 44–5

tequila 14–15, 20, 26–7, 38–9
tomatoes 30–1, 32
Tropical Rainbow 26–7

vanilla 8–9, 28–9, 52
vermouth, Appletini Mojito 18
vodka
  gazpacho 30–1
  mint and lemon grass 44–5
  nectarine and basil ice 56
  pomegranate and vanilla 28
  Raging Bull 12
  strawberry Cosmopolitan 32
  White Russian 60–1

watermelon 14–15
whiskey 36, 42, 54–5, 62–3
White Russian 60–1

yogurt
  cardamom 62–3
  preserved ginger 60–1
  rum and raisin 62–3
  White Russian 60–1